TABLE OF CONTENTS

LIST OF ILLUSTRATIONS

IT'S THE Kd, STUPID!
PRACTICAL OBSERVATIONS CONCERNING US DRUG POLICY AND PLAN COLOMBIA

United States drug policy, as delineated in the Strategic Goals and Objectives of the 2000 National Drug Control Strategy[1], contains five broad goals:

Goal 1: Educate and enable America's youth to reject illegal drugs as well as alcohol and tobacco.

Goal 2: Increase the safety of America's citizens by substantially reducing drug-related crime and violence.

Goal 3: Reduce health and social costs to the public of illegal drug use.

Goal 4: Shield America's air, land, and sea frontiers from the drug threat.

Goal 5: Break foreign and domestic drug sources cf supply.

Recently the fifth goal of this strategy resulted in $1.3 billion of military and non-military anti-drug aid being directed toward Colombia as part of the Colombian-developed plan called Plan Colombia[2]. The aid, formally announced by President Clinton during a visit to Colombia, has the primary purpose of interdicting cocaine and heroin cultivation and production at the source in Colombia.

Possible outcomes of this direct aid to Colombia will be a greater involvement in Colombia's internal revolutions and little improvement in the domestic US drug problem. Because the US military will be deeply involved should a direct intervention be necessary[3], it is worthwhile to assess the premise upon which initial US military involvement is built. This paper examines US drug policy, its flaws, and how this policy is driving the US toward violent entanglements in Colombia. This paper also argues that Plan Colombia will fail at reducing domestic drug related crime.

BACKGROUND

The United States has a drug problem. Surveys and estimates taken in the last decade of the 20th century suggest that drug use is on the upswing in the United States[4]. The 2000 Monitoring The Future Study[5], conducted in 2000, suggests that about half of all twelfth graders and alarmingly high numbers of eighth and tenth graders in the United States have tried or actively use at least one illegal drug (not including alcohol or cigarettes). The drug problem, especially the cocaine and heroin problem, is considered so serious that the Congress of the United States, along with the President, recently agreed to send $1.3 billion in military and non-military aid to Colombia to combat drug production at the source.

The aid, which includes 18 UH-60L Blackhawk and 42 UH-1N Iroquois helicopters[6], is designed to help the Colombian government in its fight against the FARC[7] (Fuerzas Armadas Revolucionarias Colombianas), ELN[8] (Ejercio de Liberacion Nacional), privately owned paramilitaries[9], and drug cartels[10] that provide the bulk of the world's cocaine and two thirds of the heroin consumed in the United States[11]. All of these groups, it should be noted, are heavily armed with advanced weaponry and are well financed by drug-derived money. The operative idea for Plan Colombia is that US military and non-military aid will allow the Colombian authorities to defoliate thousands of acres of land now under cultivation to produce drugs[12]. The idea is to make cocaine and heroin more expensive in the United States, with the hope that children and young adults who might otherwise try these drugs will be priced out of the market and will not start using them[13]. The payoff is hoped to be fewer new cocaine and heroin addicts and possibly a reduction in crime associated with the trade of these two drugs. Existing cocaine and heroin addicts will similarly see their supplies curtailed and will be forced to choose between higher prices or discontinuing their addictions.

While this hope may or may not ultimately be realized, it is instructive to look at the underpinnings of US drug policy and its application to understand why Congress and the Clinton Administration would unite on a foreign intervention fraught with peril for the US military.

US DRUG POLICY

United States drug policy seeks to accomplish five goals as stated in the introduction of this paper. The first goal seeks to stake out the moral high ground and convince and educate the youth of the United States that drug use is self-destructive and reprehensible behavior. Goals two through five target drug use and crime in its various incarnations: local violence and crime, workplace and drug treatment, trans-border, and sources of supply. These national strategy goals are premised upon the notion that crime and drugs are intertwined and that drug use and crime can in fact be severed without radical policy changes[14]. The national drug strategy visualizes a day when drug use is divorced from drug crime and when drug supply is unhinged from drug demand.

Officially, government at all levels in the United States appears to have little tolerance for illegal drugs. Numerous anti-drug programs are underway in this country. Anti-drug laws are plentiful. Drug use, possession, and distribution carry criminal penalties in most states. Drug education programs for youth abound, and drug rehabilitation programs for addicts are reasonably available for the asking[15]. But illegal drug use remains a significant problem, showing little sign of abating.

Part of the reason for the ongoing drug problem is that in practice the United States is not nearly so tough on illegal drug use as its official rhetoric. The penalties for possession of small amounts of drugs, especially for those deemed first or small time offenders, are relatively light[16][17]. Virtually unheard of is capital punishment for drug distribution. Referenda for the decriminalization of drugs or the "medical" use of illegal drugs appear at many elections, indicating a tolerance for drug use by large segments of the population. Many of the adult generation admit to using illegal drugs ranging from marijuana to heroin while in their youth. A significant number of this cohort still continue to use illegal drugs, albeit more discreetly than in their younger days.

THE REAL REASON FOR US DRUG POLICY

Illegal drug use became a significant problem in the United States during the 1960s. As can be seen from Figure 1[18], murder, robbery, and burglaries began to significantly increase at the same time that illegal drug use was entering the national conscience. While this may be a coincidence, the fact that US drug strategy clearly targets the linkage between drugs and crime further strengthens the notion that these dramatic increases in crime are, at least in part, a direct consequence of illegal drug use. While there is a moral aspect involved with the self-destruction that drug use brings to drug users, much of extant law and policy attempts to protect the non-drug using population from the murder, robbery, burglary, and larceny associated with illegal drug abuse. This notion is vividly illustrated by the fact that most of the anti-drug education programs for children are taught by police officers rather than by health or education professionals.

FIGURE 1. CRIME RATES PER 100,000 INHABITANTS FROM 1957 TO 1997

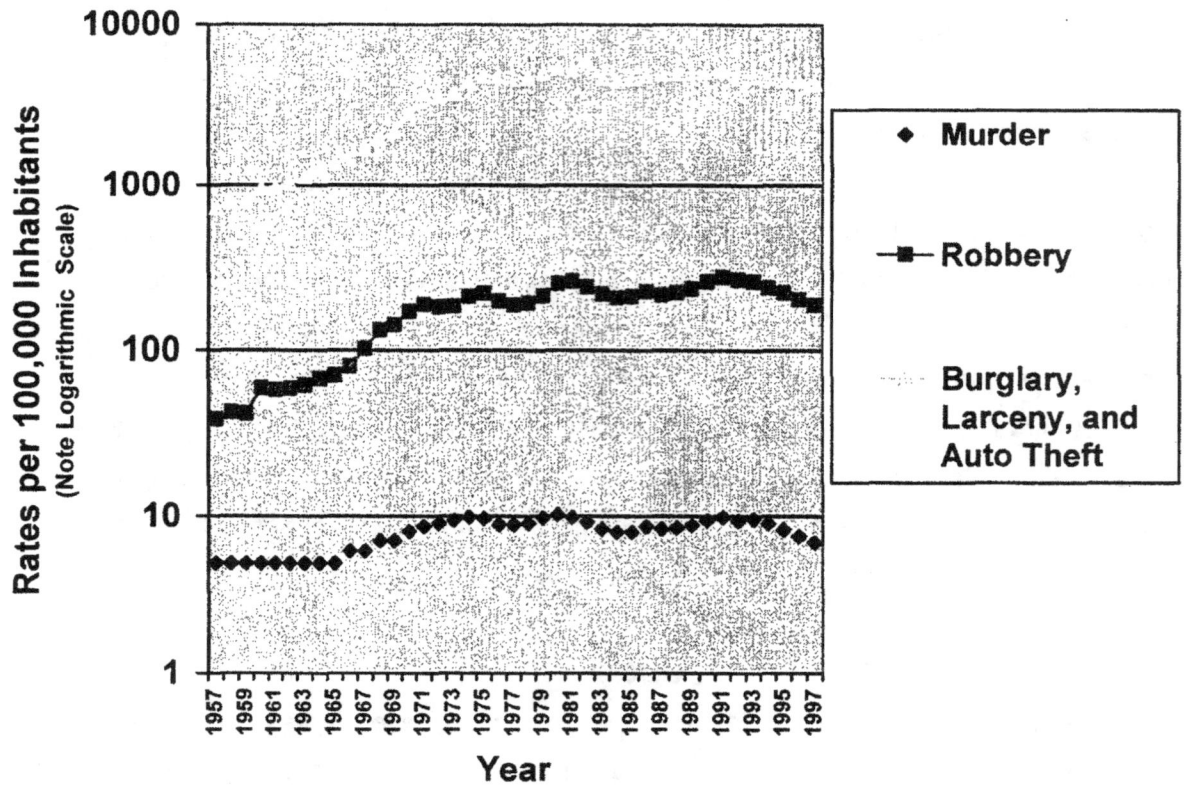

In 1957[19] the per capita rates for Murder, Robbery, and Property crime were 5, 39, and 719 incidents per 100,000 inhabitants, respectively. By 1997 the rates were 6.8, 186, and 4310, respectively. The explosion of crime has made life in the United States much more dangerous. Per capita crime rates for burglary, larceny and auto theft in 1997 were about 625% of what was experienced in the 1950s. Per capita rates for robbery were about 555% of the 1950s rates, and murder rates in 1997 were about 137% of what they were in the 1950s. One ground level observer[20] estimates that 85-90% of crime in a major east coast city is drug related. The reality of this astonishing observation has manifested itself in our drug strategy: drugs and crime are intertwined. US drug strategy in effect seeks to reduce crime by reducing drug consumption.

WHY DRUGS AND CRIME ARE INTERTWINED

Drugs and crime are intertwined for two reasons: 1) There is a demand for drugs and, 2) Drugs are illegal. Drug use carries with it rewards for both the user and the drug dealer. The drug user seeks the pleasurable feelings associated with drug use. The drug dealer seeks the monetary profit realized by selling drugs. Because the sale and use of illegal drugs is, by definition, illegal, the entire transaction takes place outside of normally applied regulatory provisions and the law.

These forces alone -demand and profit- would be sufficient to propel an industry, much like demand and profit propel industries in sectors as diverse as chocolate and literature. But the drug trade has another formidable weapon in its arsenal. That weapon is drug addiction. The pleasurable feeling that initially rewards illegal drug use rapidly becomes the user's *raison d'etre*.

The craving of the drug addict for more drugs knows no rest. The media is replete with tragic stories of cocaine addicts who lie, cheat, steal, and sell themselves or their children, to get their next fix. In practical terms, this means the addict is willing to pay money -lots of money- for the drugs consumed. Drug traffickers exist to fill this demand.

The drug trade is extremely lucrative. US drug laws make production, distribution and use of drugs such as cocaine and heroin illegal. Stiff penalties may be imposed on those convicted of such offenses, yet the drug trade flourishes in spite of these laws because suppliers make enormous profits. This trade is conducted outside the law and is free from government taxation, regulation, and oversight. Organized crime is heavily involved. Addicts have little choice but to pay the going rate and to expose themselves to the violence associated with the drug trade. Certainly there are 'business' problems and setbacks for drug dealers, as rival drug dealers often resolve disputes at the end of a gun, but by and large, there is no shortage of volunteers to fill the shoes of the most recently deceased dealer. Why? In a word, money.

THE BIOCHEMISTRY OF DRUG ADDICTION

When considering US drug policy, it may be instructive to examine the metabolic pathways that illegal drugs activate to produce the feeling of euphoria and, eventually, addiction. For non-addicts, it is difficult to understand the power of the forces that are unleashed by addiction to drugs such as cocaine and heroin. The biochemistry of addiction is only beginning to be understood, but what is known is enlightening. Cocaine addiction is discussed to illustrate this point.

The pleasurable feeling resulting from cocaine use has been described as a very long and intense orgasm[21]. Whatever the feeling is like, it is clear that cocaine users find it exquisitely pleasurable. So what's going on at a molecular level to account for this? The active ingredient of coca is the cocaine molecule. The cocaine molecule has two important properties. First, it easily crosses the blood brain barrier, so it can quickly gain access to the chemistry of the brain, and second, it has the unique ability to bind to a naturally occurring neural molecule called the Dopamine Transporter Molecule[22].

Current thinking is that by binding to the Dopamine Transporter Molecule, the cocaine molecule reduces the ability of the Transporter Molecule to bind Dopamine[23]. Dopamine is a molecule that is released in the brain in response to stimuli normally associated with feelings of intense pleasure[24]. Dopamine itself is not responsible for the pleasurable feelings, but is part of a cascade of biochemical reactions that ultimately do result in the pleasurable feeling. The Dopamine Transporter Molecule's role in a normal brain is to bind up Dopamine and essentially take it out of circulation[25].

In a normally functioning brain, a stimulus causes Dopamine to be released. A cascade of other biochemical reactions then occurs, with the end result being a pleasurable feeling. The brain controls this process by having the Dopamine Transporter Molecule sop up free Dopamine molecules. By taking Dopamine out of circulation the cascade is effectively stopped and the pleasurable feeling comes to an end. Cocaine short circuits this process by preventing the Dopamine Transporter Molecule from sopping up free Dopamine molecules. This allows the biochemical cascade to continue much longer than would occur in a normal brain, with a concomitantly much longer and more intensely pleasurable feeling. While this description is a gross simplification of the neurochemistry associated with cocaine[26], it illustrates the point that there are basic molecular principles involved concerning cocaine use.

The mere binding of the cocaine molecule to the Dopamine Transporter Molecule does not cause a person to become addicted to cocaine in and of itself. Addiction to cocaine is thought to come about because the brain has the ability to remember drug induced stimuli and the resulting pleasurable sensations. How this happens is not clear, and there are several competing explanations. It is clear, however, *that there is a molecular basis for addiction*[27]. That is, the basis of addiction is rooted in chemical reactions and the brain's control of these reactions. Older hypotheses that attributed addiction to character weakness or lack of self-control, while explaining the overt manifestations of the addiction, often did not address the chemical circuitry of the brain. In any event, it is clear that an intense craving is established in addicts that drive them to seek and use more cocaine. This craving is ultimately based on the binding of the cocaine molecule.

Kd (pronounced Kay-Dee) is the molecular biologist's shorthand for the disassociation constant of a small molecule binding to a larger molecule[28]. The disassociation constant is a measure of how tightly two molecules bind together. Molecules that only bind loosely together have high Kds (they disassociate easily). Those that bind tightly together have low Kds (they do not disassociate easily). The human brain is a veritable soup of different molecules. Most have high Kds for each other. That is, they bump into each other and no binding occurs.

Molecules that are part of biochemical pathways almost always have Kds that are low enough so as to make the binding reactions specific. For whatever reason, be it a joke of nature, an accident, or just random chance, the coca plant produces a molecule (cocaine) that binds with a low enough Kd to the Dopamine Transporter Molecule to short circuit normal brain chemistry. Man, with his ever inquisitive mind, discovered this fact, and has been cultivating coca ever since. The ultimate biological result of this Kd is addiction. The economic result of this Kd is profit for drug cartels and economic hardship for users and the victims of crimes committed to generate the money needed to buy drugs.

Nature endowed the human race with the predisposition to reproduce. One of the inducements for reproduction is the pleasurable feeling of orgasm associated with the sex act. This is no accident. One can conjecture that if copulation were immediately associated with intense pain or gut wrenching sickness (pregnancy and giving birth excepted), that the human race would have become extinct long ago. If cocaine use short-circuits the brain's chemistry to produce an orgasmic feeling or something like it, it should be clear to all that we are dealing with a very powerful force.

The 2000 National Drug Control Strategy essentially overlooks the fact that cocaine and other drug use can permanently alter the chemistry of the brain[29]. The strategy contains five broad goals broken down into 31 objectives. Only one of the 31 objectives, goal three, objective five, addresses research into the mechanisms of drug addiction, whereas seven objectives deal with drug education in its various incarnations and ten objectives deal in one form or another with interdicting drug production at its source. In the more detailed explanation of the goals and objectives research into the mechanisms of drug addiction is not mentioned[30].

The National Drug Control Strategy endorses treatment for addiction, about which it says can be successful initially, but which is also a chronic relapsing disorder[31]. Many of the treatment programs amount to counseling and voluntary cessation of drug use. Various studies[32][33][34][35][36] indicate recidivism rates for cocaine and heroin addicts range from about 50% to 80%. That recidivism rates are high given counseling based treatment regimes is not cause for wonder. If the host of diseases that physicians deal with everyday which also are due to changes in metabolic pathways were to be treated in the same way, we could reasonably expect mortality rates in the US to be significantly higher. Imagine the results if counseling based therapy were applied to metabolic diseases such as type I diabetes (The diabetic's body makes little or no insulin. Treatment is by insulin injection). Type I diabetics cannot "think" or will themselves well.

When all is said and done, the Kd of the cocaine molecule certainly invokes one of the most sought after feelings in the world, be it a super orgasm or something better. This is certainly part of the feeling the cocaine addict craves and seeks, and, of course, the drug cartels take full advantage of this phenomenon. At the end of the day, it is drug consumption, not drug production, which drives the drug trade and its associated violence.

US DRUG POLICY AND COLOMBIA

Focus now on cocaine and heroin. Cocaine and heroin addicts demand cocaine and heroin. They are willing to pay for these drugs. They are willing to risk their lives buying, taking, and selling these drugs. They know intellectually that there are great risks associated with these drugs. In their more lucid moments, they acknowledge these realities, but they still use drugs. This creates demand. As long as there is a demand, someone will fill the demand if a profit can be made. As it turns out for most of the world, at least when talking about cocaine and to some degree heroin, the drug cartels of Colombia now fill that demand.

For years there have been calls to do something about the drug problem in the United States, and especially about the drug problem among the nation's youth. Most of the recent past youth-oriented programs have been either ineffectual or have at best held the line on drug use, even when judged by the government's own drug use statistics[37]. During the Clinton administration, drug strategy gradually shifted from interdicting the transport of drugs to interdicting the supply of drugs at the source. That such a strategy was even contemplated was due to the convergence of cocaine and to a lesser extent heroin production in Colombia. If this convergence had not taken place, it is unlikely that such a strategy could have been formulated. In any event, the at-the-source interdiction strategy of the United States now focuses primarily on Colombia as evidenced by the $1.3B in aid approved for Plan Colombia.

RISKS OF US MILITARY INTERVENTION IN COLOMBIA

National leaders have taken pains[38] to present the $1.3B in aid to Colombia as a drug interdiction strategy and not as a US military intervention aimed at propping up the failing Colombian government. Justly deserved or not, the strategy has reminded many of the US entrance into the Vietnam War[39]. The parallels are ample: the drug gangs, the communist revolution, the corruption of the Colombian government, the domino effect of narcotics cultivation in neighboring countries, and herbicide defoliation.

Colombia has no corner on the market for land suitable for the cultivation of coca[40] and poppy. If we somehow do succeed in removing the coca fields from the equation (a big if), then the cartels and growers may simply remove operations to, for example, Bolivia, Peru, or perhaps even in the United States. It is also entirely possible that such a move may make the supply problem worse, as drug producers will almost certainly develop alternative technological solutions.

Consider for a moment the scenario where the drug cartels hire the technical expertise to develop a bulk cocaine production facility, producing pure cocaine hydrochloride (HCl) much after the methods of pharmaceutical companies at the turn of the last century when cocaine was legal[41] [42]. This scenario bypasses the need for farmers to grow coca and could be easily hidden. This scenario is essentially what has happened with methamphetamine. Ingenious drug traffickers figured out how to set up numerous small-scale laboratories that are difficult for authorities to detect. The end-result being that there is no shortage of methamphetamine despite law enforcement efforts.

AID TO COLOMBIA

The US is already deeply involved in Colombia. We have between 150 and 300 US military personnel in Colombia at any one time, although they are not concentrated in one location[43]. The insertion of advanced helicopters materially changes our relationship with Colombia, and with every new materiel transfer we bind ourselves closer to the Colombians. Metaphorically, our Kd for a Colombian war becomes smaller.

As Congress debated the Colombian aid package, the discussion initially, centered on whether or not to send new or surplus (UH-1N = new, UH-1H = surplus) helicopters to Colombia. US helicopter manufacturers joined in the debate, with vigorous lobbying efforts[44] to promote helicopters they produced. The debate was eventually enlarged to include sending the UH-60L. Numerous sound reasons were put forth to send the UH-60L, including the facts that the UH-60L is very capable at high altitude and is very survivable under fire, and, the positive message that sending our best helicopter would give to the Colombians. Eventually it was decided that a mix of helicopters, 42 UH-1Ns and 18 UH-60Ls would be sent, sent that is, after they rolled off the production lines in 2001. Some of these 'aid' helicopters still had to be manufactured[45]. In reality, the bulk of the 'aid' to Colombia will be spent in the United States and the products procured from the aid money will then be given to Colombia.

Although the US helicopter donations to the Colombians are supposed to be used solely to facilitate the eradication of the coca and poppy fields, and not to conduct combat operations against the FARC and ELN, all of the helicopters will be armed, as it is unlikely the FARC, ELN, private paramilitaries, and the drug cartels will stand idly by and allow their businesses to be destroyed in respect of this US-imposed restriction. The US will also supply the ammunition for the armaments, because Colombia lacks the infrastructure to manufacture the ammunition internally. The US will also have to supply armorers to maintain the weapons, because the chosen weapons are no ordinary helicopter mounted machine guns, but rather are the half million dollar-a-copy GAU/19A .50 caliber gun[46]. Because the GAU/19A is an advanced weapon, the US will have to train the Colombian door gunners to use it. And of course, in order to use the GAU/19A it has to be mounted on a flying helicopter, so the US will have to train the pilots of the helicopters. To fly the helicopters the US will have to maintain (at least initially) the helicopters and supply them with parts, because, again, Colombia does not presently possess this capability. Add some night vision devices (which the US will have to supply, maintain, and train) into the mix because it will rapidly become too dangerous to

10

fly[47] during the day when the bad guys start to use shoulder fired surface-to-air missiles. (A partially completed submarine, capable of hauling 200 tons of drugs was recently discovered in Colombia. This level of sophistication suggests surface to air missiles will not be hard to obtain[48].) Figure on a continuation of US intelligence aircraft for target location, and pretty soon we have a Colombian military counter drug unit (the goal is a brigade size formation[49]) that is supplied, trained, maintained, and perhaps even partially directed by the United States. Direction, whether partial or total may or may not occur, but one must consider that, for the receiving country, it is sometimes difficult to say no when survival depends on aid from the United States.

While this may all be great for the bottom line of US industry, as most of these services will be supplied or contracted out to industry, it is not great for the United States Army. The US Army is already training the Colombian Army[50]. It is already flying the intelligence aircraft that find and target the fields[51]. It is already supplying arms and other equipment. Now it will supply more hardware and more people to maintain the hardware. No matter that these Americans are active duty military or contractors to the State Department, the result will be more Americans directly exposed to the dangers of Colombia.

If the cartels, FARC, ELN, and paramilitaries have or acquire surface-to-air missiles, anti-drug missions will be forced to fly at night to avoid detection by visual tracking systems, unless additional sophisticated aircraft survivability equipment is provided to the Colombians. Night flight in the mountains of Colombia will require the use of night vision devices to be effective, as night mountain flying is some of the most hazardous flying of all. Using night vision devices while flying a helicopter is not a trivial task. The US Army, which pioneered flight with night vision goggles, prescribes at least 20 hours of flight training to become night vision qualified. Night vision qualification is merely a license to learn. Experienced night vision goggle pilots have several hundred hours of night vision goggle time. High levels of goggle time usually take years to accumulate. This steep learning curve puts added pressure on the US to speed up the process by having US pilots fly with Colombian pilots. That this is not such an extreme notion is illustrated by the fact that US pilots are already flying the intelligence mission and US contract pilots are flying many of the crop dusting missions.

There is also a practical side to this Colombian adventure. Whether we admit it or not, we are willingly subjecting our forces to the acidic, corrosive effects of the drug trade. It is not impossible for some of our folks to sell out to the other side given the

11

amounts of cash available for bribery and corruption. Indeed, it has already happened. No less than the US Commander of the anti-drug unit in Bogotá (in jail) and his wife (in jail) succumbed to the siren call of cocaine[52]. If we send more Americans to Colombia, we should expect more sell-outs from our own people.

Finally, a thought about the FARC and ELN. Both of these revolutionary groups have been waging war against the Colombian government for over forty years[53][54]. Waging a struggle for forty years suggests that these groups are seriously dedicated to their stated goals of revolution. The last time the US was involved with a group that possessed a similar fervor was in Vietnam, where, admittedly, we seriously misjudged the staying power and the dedication to task these types of Marxist groups possess.

PREDICTIONS

> Making predictions is tricky business, especially when you're talking about the future.
>
> —Yogi Berra

Predicting the future of issues as complex as the US drug problem and Plan Colombia are fraught with peril. Yet, experience suggests that we should examine the potential outcomes of a strategy for its second and third order effects. These might include:

-Plan Colombia will reduce the production of cocaine and heroin in Colombia but overall flow of cocaine and heroin into the US will not be substantially curtailed. The cartels will shift production to other countries not covered by Plan Colombia, despite the replacement crop aid provided to neighboring countries, and will invest in synthetic processes to produce cocaine. The two year lead time between announcement of Plan Colombia and crop eradication in earnest will allow the cartels sufficient time to make necessary changes.

-Drug crime rates (at least those attributed to cocaine and heroin) in the US will not substantially change due to Plan Colombia. The current purity of cocaine and heroin is such that one use is often sufficient to produce an addiction. This purity ensures a continuing supply of new addicts. A continuing supply of addicts ensures a continuing demand. Demand usually, judging from the past, ensures a continuing supply of drugs. Availability of drugs usually results in drug-crime.

-Drug cartels and/or the FARC and/or the ELN and/or the para-militaries will conduct successful attacks on US personnel in attempts to break the US political will to remain in Colombia. FARC strength alone is estimated at over 15,000 personnel. These well-armed groups have conducted attacks and raids throughout Colombia in the past, and there is no reason to suspect they will not do the same in the future.

-More US aid will be required for Plan Colombia to be successful. Sixty helicopters in a country the size of Texas will not prove sufficient to the task. Helicopters will be lost through error and attack, and some part of the $1.3B will be wasted or siphoned-off.

SUMMING UP

The view of this author is that Plan Colombia is probably better for Colombia than for the United States. Colombia is interested in reasserting control over all its territory and suppressing the various revolutionary groups it is now in contest with. The United States is interested in solving its internal drug problem.

Plan Colombia helps Colombia because it goes after the economic support of the revolutionary groups and the drug cartels. If the cocaine money dries up, so does the ability of these groups to wage revolution. This part of the plan makes economic sense and will probably succeed.

Plan Colombia does not help the United States to the same degree because it seeks to destroy only *Colombia's* cocaine and heroin production capacity. Little is done to prevent a shift in production to other Latin American countries or to synthetic methods. Plan Colombia certainly does little to curtail US demand. A lucrative demand such as the drug trade will not exist in a vacuum. Whether, in this case, it is filled by a shift in production to other countries or a shift to synthetic production, the demand will be filled.

Because drugs and crime are closely intertwined, it is unlikely that Plan Colombia will have the desired impact on the United States. Crime and drug use rates attributed to cocaine and heroin are unlikely to significantly change unless the supply of cocaine and heroin is curtailed and these drugs are just not available at any price anywhere. Plan Colombia is unlikely to result in so favorable a situation.

At the end of the day it's not the Colombian farmer that is giving us trouble, and it's not the cartels, as ruthless and despicable as they are. It is the demand in our own country that is causing the crime and self-destruction of our citizens. The Kd of cocaine drives craziness. The Kd drives demand. It's the Kd, stupid!

WORD COUNT = 5090

ENDNOTES

[1] Office of National Drug Control Policy; Strategic Goals and Objectives of the 2000 National Drug Control Strategy, available from <http://www.whitehousedrugpolicy.gov/ndcs00/chap1.html>; Internet; accessed 22 January 2001. The five goals are organized with multiple objectives for each goal. Interestingly, the goals and objectives are expressed as platitudes, such as "Shield America's air, land, and sea frontiers from the drug threat". In general, no metrics define what success might be for a particular goal.

[2] Tod Robberson, "Clinton launches Colombia aid plan: 'This is not Vietnam,' president says," The Dallas Morning News, 31 August 2000, p. 1A. President Clinton, under the absolute highest security, swept into Colombia, made his announcements, talked with local officials, and promptly departed.

[3] Associated Press, "Colombian Rebels Vow To Hit U.S. Advisors," The Chicago Tribune, 2 October 2000, p.5. U.S. troops, particularly special forces and intelligence troops, have been training the Colombian Army with the goal of forming a brigade size anti-drug unit.

[4] National Institute on Drug Abuse, INFOFAX National Trends 13567; available from <http://www.drugabuse gov/infofax/nationaltrends.html>, Internet; accessed 27 October 2000. Drug use has fluctuated higher and lower over the last forty years. In 1996 there were an estimated 13 million illicit drug users in the US, up from about 12.8 million the year before.

[5] National Institute on Drug Abuse, High School and Youth Trends 13565; available from <http://www.drugabuse.gov/infofax/infofaxindex.html>. Internet; accessed 23 January 2001. The survey suggests that in 1999 about 54% of the nations 12th graders had used an illegal drug at least once (not including tobacco and alcohol). This number was up from about 46% of the nations 12th graders in 1994. Similar trends were seen for 8th and 10th graders.

[6] Eric Schmitt, "$1.3 Billion Voted To Fight Drug War Among Colombians", The New York Times, 30 June 2000, sec. A, p. 1. These aircraft were picked both for political reasons and for their ability to fly in the mountains of Colombia.

[7] Robberson. The Marxist led FARC has been battling the Colombian government for over 40 years.

[8] ELN Colombia Homepage. Available from< http://www.web.net/eln/>; Internet; accessed 27 January 2001. This site provides an overview of the ELN, its Maoist roots, and its goals for Colombia.

[9] Dan Gardner, "How 'victory' in the Drug War has left Colombia in ruins: the U.S. boasted that defeating Colombia's cartels would end the illegal drug trade. Instead, things got worse," The Ottawa Citizen, 6 September 2000, p. A1. The paramilitaries are often responsible for human rights violations and are employed by rich landowners and drug traffickers.

[10] Ibid. Pablo Escobar, head of the Medellin cartel was hunted and killed in 1993. Since then, the Cali cartel has blossomed along with numerous other cartels.

[11] Ibid. Colombia's entry into the heroin market came as a result of collusion between the Asian heroin traffickers and the Colombian cartels.

[12] Pedro Ruz Gutierrez and E.A. Torriero, "Outsourcing the Drug War," The Orlando Sentinel, 19 September 2000. p. A1. The poppy and coca fields are often located high in the Colombian mountains and are often vigorously defended. The helicopters are used to carry troops and to suppress defensive fires, while crop dusters dispense herbicides on the fields.

[13] The ideas in this paragraph are based on remarks made by a former US government official speaking at the USAWC. The speaker expressed the hope that once drug prices reached some (unstated) amount, that children would be priced out of the market and would never make that first drug purchase. The speaker recognized that current addicts, if Plan Colombia is successful, would have to raise more money to support their habits.

[14] Office of National Drug Control Policy. Goal Two, Increase the safety of America's citizens by substantially reducing drug-related crime and violence, has five objectives. Objective number four is "Break the cycle of drug abuse and crime". The existence of this goal and objective implies that within the current climate of drugs being declared illegal, that breaking this cycle is somehow possible.

[15] National Institute on Drug Abuse, INFOFAX Treatment Trends 13569; available from <http://www.drugabuse.gov/infofax/treatmenttrends.html>, Internet; accessed 27 October 2000. In 1995 there were 1.9 million admissions to publicly funded substance abuse treatment programs.

[16] H.G. Reza, "Drug Runners Arrested at Border Often Go Free; Smuggling: Crackdown Leads to More Seizures, but Jail Overcrowding and Clashing Priorities Force Suspects' Release," The Los Angeles Times, May 12, 1996, p 1. In this case, then Attorney General Reno opined that these individuals were indeed punished, as their boarder crossing cards were confiscated.

[17] Robert C. Bonner, "Clinton's Flawed Drug-Smuggling Policy", San Diego Union-Tribune, June 4, 1996. According to then Attorney General Reno, the criterion of leniency for Mexicans trying to cross the US boarder and being caught with under 125 pounds of marijuana applies. If you are smuggling "only" 100 pounds, you do not meet the criteria for prosecution, unless you are a US citizen. Reno also says that there must also be sufficient "evidence" of knowledge and intent for prosecution.

[18] Kurian, George, Datapedia of the United States 1790-2000, (Lanham, MD: Bernan Press, 1994), p. 155. It is interesting to note that the Clinton Administration routinely used data that only extended back to 1973, ignoring the tremendous rises in crime that occurred starting in the 1960s. Further, starting in 1992 (the beginning of the Clinton administration) the Department of Justice changed the methodology of how crime statistics are compiled and reported. The DOJ went so far as to publish a statistic with the amazing title " Violent crime rates have declined since 1994, reaching the lowest

level ever recorded in 1999", (http://www.ojp.usdoj.gov/bjs/glance/viort.html, accessed 27 October 2000) completely ignoring violent crime rates that were on the order of one-fifth in the 1950s of what they are in 1997.

[19] Ibid., 156.

[20] Unnamed (by request) Baltimore City Police Officer, interviewed by author, 28 September 2000, Bel Air, Maryland. This officer has worked counter narcotic operations for over 20 years and estimates "At least 85-90% of all crime in Baltimore is drug related."

[21] Adrienne M. Carver, "Cocaine Addiction," No date; available from <http://academic.uofs.edu/student/carvera2/paper.htm>; Internet; accessed 30 September 2000. Carver summarizes numerous sites that speak of the effects of cocaine.

[22] Michael Balter, "New Clues to Brain Dopamine Control, Cocaine Addiction," Science 271 (16 February 1996): 909. Bolter summarizes work done by Marc Caror et al. of Duke University and others, that provide a view of the molecular mechanisms of cocaine addiction.

[23] Ibid. Amphetamines may act in the same way.

[24] Ingrid Wickelgren, "Getting the Brain's Attention," Science 278 (3 October 1997): 35. How this happens is still unclear.

[25] Balter, 909, Available evidence suggests this to be the case. Neurobiology is very complex, and the final answer may turn out differently.

[26] Wickelgren, 35. Dopamine is thought by some to be the molecule used by the brain to facilitate learning by drawing attention to new or unusual stimuli. It is clear, however, that Dopamine is associated with cocaine use and addiction in some form.

[27] Eric J. Nestler and George K. Aghajanian, "Molecular and Cellular Basis of Addiction." Science 278 (3 October 1997): 58-63. Addiction seems to have at least two parts: the stimuli that cause intense pleasure and a resulting change in neural circuits from repetitive use of the drug.

[28] David Freifelder, Physical Biochemistry: Applications to Biochemistry and Molecular Biology (New York: Freeman and Company, 1982), 655. Formalized by the equation $Kd=[P][A]/[PA]$ where $[P]$ is the concentration of a macromolecule that has a single binding site, $[A]$ is the concentration of a small molecule and $[PA]$ is the concentration of the small molecule and large molecules bound together.

[29] Alan I. Leshner, "Addiction is a Brain Disease, and It Matters," Science 278 (3 October 1997): 45-47. Leshner argues that repetitive drug use essentially throws a genetic switch in the brain that results in addictive behavior. Metabolic pathways are activated and genes are expressed that are normally tightly regulated. These changes may be, essentially, permanent.

[30] Office of National Drug Control Policy, Annual Report and the National Drug Control Strategy: An Overview, No date; available from <http://www.whitehousedrugpolicy.gov/policy/ndcs00 /chap1.html>; Internet; accessed 15 January 2001. This document gives an overview of what each goal is supposed to accomplish.

[31] Ibid. Under the heading "Overview of the National Drug Control Strategy" the statement is made that "Research clearly demonstrates that treatment works". Further on in the overview, under the heading "Goal 3: Reduce health and social costs to the public of illegal drug use" the somewhat contrary statement is made that "Drug dependence is a chronic, relapsing disorder that exacts an enormous cost on individuals".

[32] Patrick Zickler, "High-Dose Methadone Improves Treatment Outcomes," NIDA Notes 14-5 (No date): available from <http://www.drugabuse.gov/Nida_notes/nnvol14n5/highdose.html>; Internet; accessed 27 October 2000. Zickler summarizes the work of Dr. Eric Strain, of the Johns Hopkins University Medical Center, where positive outcomes in this study on methadone replacement therapy were defined as using opiates no more than once per week and one third of the patients remaining in treatment during a phase out of the methadone treatment.

[33] Patrick Zickler, "Combining Drug Counseling Methods Proves Effective In Treating Cocaine Addiction" NIDA Notes 14-5 (No date): available from <http://www.drugabuse.gov/Nida_notes/nnvol1 4n5/combining.html>; Internet; accessed 27 October 2000. Zickler summarizes work at several university and hospital sites that combined individual and group counseling. "Successful" results were noted in that 38% of patients that completed the combined counseling therapy remained cocaine free during a three-month period ending nine months after the counseling was completed.

[34]Steven Stocker, "Men and Women in Drug Abuse Treatment Relapse at Different Rates and for Different Reasons," NIDA Notes 13-4 (No date): available from <http://www.drugabuse.gov /Nida_notes/nnvol13n/relapse.html>; Internet; accessed 27 October 2000. Stocker summarizes work performed by Dr. Robert Fiorentine, UCLA, that compared male and female cocaine and marijuana relapse rates after six months of individual, group, and family counseling and education. Men relapsed (use drugs three or more times per week) at about a 78% rate. Women relapse at about a 68% rate.

[35] Patrick Zickler, "Coping Skills Help Patients Recognize and Resist The Urge to Use Cocaine," NIDA Notes 13-6 (No date): available from<http://www.drugabuse.gov/Nida_notes/nnvol13n6 /coping.html>; Internet; accessed 27 October 2000. Zickler summarizes work by Dr. Rohsenow et al., of Brown University, that provides cocaine-specific coping skills treatment to addicts. About 45% of the group relapsed after treatment, but average days of drug use were 6.2 days compared to 13+ days for a control group.

[36]Barbara Shine, "Some Cocaine Abusers Fare Better With Cognitive-Behavioral Therapy, Others With 12-Step Program," NIDA Notes 15-1 (No date): available from<http://www.drugabuse.gov/ Nida_notes/nnvol15n1/cocaine.html>; Internet; accessed 27 October 2000. Shine summarizes work of Dr. Hall, UCSF, which compared

cognitive-behavioral therapy with the 12-step facilitation method. Forty-six percent of the cognitive-behavioral therapy group remained drug free for one month, while 54% of the 12-step group remained drug free for one month. Various differences emerged indicating one method over the other if considering ability to reason abstractly or religiosity.

[37] National Institute on Drug Abuse, High School and Youth Trends 13565.   The monitoring the Future Study shows that drug use for 8th graders has remained from 1994 to 2000 essentially constant, ranging from about 26% to about 31%. 10th grader drug use has risen from about 37% in 1994 to about 45% in 2000, and 12th grader drug use has risen from about 47% in 1994 to about 54% in 2000.

[38]Robberson. "A condition of this aid is that we are not going to get into a shooting war, this is not Vietnam, Neither is it Yankee imperialism." Said President Clinton in his eight-hour trip to Cartagena that was marked with extraordinary security including rings of troops around the city and submarine patrols.

[39]David Nyhan, " Colombia drug war: it's Vietnam all over again," The Montrea Gazette, 13 July 2000, Editorial/Op-ed, p. B3. Nyhan's title says it all.

[40]Drug Enforcement Administration Intelligence Division, Strategic Intelligence Coca Cultivation and Cocaine Processing: An Overview, September 1993, available from <http://www.druglibrary.org /schaffer govpubs/cocccp.htm>; Internet; accessed 11 February 2001 To quote from the Executive Summary: "It has been estimated that there are over 200 Erythroxylum species growing in the Western Hemisphere. Only 17 species can be utilized to produce cocaine. Fifteen of the 17 species contain relatively low levels of cocaine alkaloid and subsequently are not cultivated. In South America two species and two varieties within each of these species are cultivated. They are:

--E. coca Species var. coca and var. ipadu

--E. novogranatense Species var. novogranatense and var. truxillense

These varieties are traditionally cultivated in the following areas:

--Bolivia

E. coca var. coca

--Peru

E. coca var. coca

E. novogranatense var. truxillense

E. coca var. ipadu

--Colombia

E. novogranatense var. novogranatense

E. coca var. ipadu

E. novogranatense var. truxillense

The most widely grown variety of coca is E. coca var. coca which is cultivated on the eastern slope of the Andes from Bolivia in the south to as far north as central Ecuador. This area of the Andes has a tropical climate and experiences high amounts of rainfall. Coca in this region is usually grown between 1,650 and 4,950 feet in elevation. E. novogranatense var. novogranatense thrives in the drier regions of Colombia and, to a lesser extent, Venezuela. It is also grown at lower elevations where the climate is generally hotter. The main variety of E.novogranatense, var. truxillense, is grown up to an elevation of 4,950 feet. The last variety, E. coca var. ipadu, is found in southern Colombia, northeastern Peru, and western Brazil in the Amazon basin. E. coca var. ipadu is primarily cultivated by Indians for their own consumption and is not as high in cocaine alkaloids as the other three."

[41]The Drugs Guide, Cocaine History 02: "oh that craving," available from <http://www.seethru. co.uk/drugs/cocaine/12 history02.htm>; Internet; accessed 11 February 2001. This site reports that in 1900 European and US pharmaceutical companies were synthetically producing ton quantities of pure cocaine HCl.

[42] Cocaine Synthesis Notes, available from <http://leda.lycaeum.org/Documents/ Cocaine_Synthesis_Notes.12948.shtml>; Internet; accessed 11 February 2001. This Internet site, as do many others, provides a detailed recipe for the synthesis of cocaine. It also provides procedures for the synthesis of precursor chemicals that may be difficult to obtain.

[43] The ideas in this paragraph are based on remarks made by a former government official speaking at the USAWC. US forces in Colombia are consciously spread out to avoid presenting lucrative targets.

[44]Tim Golden, "Colombia and Copters and Clash Over Choice," The New York Times, 6 March 2000, sec A, p. 6. Bell Helicopter Textron, the maker of the UH-1N, and United Technologies, the maker of the UH-60L, made the rounds to various elected officials. These officials took up the cause based, Golden argues, on where the helicopters were manufactured.

[45] Associated Press, "Budget Deal May Delay Helicopters For Colombia," The Dallas Morning News, 22 September 2000. The delivery of the helicopters by the manufacturers is contingent upon money being made available in the federal budget, and may not actually occur until 2003.

[46]Jerry Seper, "Big Guns Are Back In Aerial Drug War," The Washington Times, 21 September 2000, p. 8. The Colombian police used the GAU/19A, with much trouble. When the weapons failed to work, the US manufacturer, General Dynamics, was called to repair them, as the Colombians did not have the ability to repair the weapons themselves.

[47] Jared Kotler, "Military Suffers Heavy Losses in Colombia Fighting," The Associated Press, 20 October 2000, available from <http://ap.com/ap/breaking/mga3cxfqkec.html>; Internet; accessed 22 October 2000. Kotler reports on three days of fighting between the FARC and the Colombian military. In all, he reports that 54 soldiers and police were killed and that a Blackhawk was downed by suspected rebel fire.

[48] Underwater Operations," The Associated Press, 7 September 2000. Available from <http://www.abcnews.go.com/sections/world/dailynews/colombia000907.html >; Internet; accessed 1 October 2000. This report details the finding of a submarine capable of carrying 200 tons of drugs. The sub was discovered while still under construction. Smaller, functional submarines have also been recovered.

[49] The ideas in this paragraph are based on remarks made by a former government official speaking at the USAWC. The US is currently training two battalion-sized units.

[50] Ibid. The cap on US military is supposed to be between 300 and 500 persons deployed to Colombia.

[51] Pedro Ruz Gutierrez and E.A. Torriero, "U.S. Aid Bill For Colombia Creates Jitters," The Orlando Sun-Sentinel, 2 July 2000, p. 1A. In 1999 a US Army Intel gathering aircraft crashed, killing all five crewmembers. The official Army version attributes the cause to pilot error. Others attribute the cause to a rebel surface to air missile.

[52] Jane McHugh, "FIRED," The Army Times, 20 November 2000, p. 8. US Army Colonel Fred Hiett, former commander of the US Army's anti-drug operation in Bogotá, pleaded guilty to money laundering and related charges and was sentenced to five months behind bars and five months home detention. COL Hiett apparently was not using illegal drugs. However, COL Hiett's wife, Laurie, was using cocaine, and was smuggling the drug back into the United States.

[53]ELN Colombia Homepage.

[54] Robberson.

BIBLIOGRAPHY

Baltimore City Police Officer interviewed by author, requesting anonymity, 28
    September 2000, Bel Air, MD.

Balter, Michael. "New Clues to Brain Dopamine Control, Cocaine Addiction."
    <u>Science</u> 271 (16 February 1996): 909.

Bonner, Robert C. "Clinton's Flawed Drug-Smuggling Policy." <u>San Diego Union-Tribune</u>,
    June 4, 1996.

"Budget Deal May Delay Helicopters For Colombia." Associated Press, <u>The Dallas
    Morning News</u>, 22 September 2000.

Carver, Adrienne M. "Cocaine Addiction." No date. Available from<http://academic.
    uofs.edu/student/ carvera2/paper.html>. Internet. Accessed 30 September 2000.

"Cocaine Synthesis Notes." No date. Available from <http://leda.lycaeum.org/
    Documents/Cocaine_Synthesis_Notes.12948.shtml>. Internet. Accessed 11
    February 2001.

"Colombian Rebels Vow To Hit U.S. Advisors." Associated Press, <u>The Chicago Tribune</u>,
    2 October 2000, p.5.

Curtis, Henry Pierson. "Florida's Heroin Connection; Virtually all of the heroin that
    reaches central Florida comes from Colombia, a rugged country bigger than
    Texas, where billionaire drug lords and guerrilla armies have fought for years and
    35,000 civilians have died in the past decade." <u>The Orlando Sentinel</u>, 28 March
    1999, sec A, p.1.

DeYoung, Karen. "U.S. Colonel to plead guilty in Colombia Drug Probe." <u>Washington
    Post,</u> 4 April 2000, p. 1.

Drugs Guide, The, <u>Cocaine History 02: "oh that craving."</u> No date. Available from <<u>http://www. seethru.co.uk/drugs/cocaine/12_history02.htm</u>>. Internet. Accessed 11 February 2001.

Ejercio de Liberacion Nacional Homepage. No date. Available from <<u>http://www.web.net/eln/</u>>. Internet. Accessed 27 January 2001.

Freifelder, David. <u>Physical Biochemistry: Applications to Biochemistry and Molecular Biology</u> (New York: Freeman and Company, 1982.), p.655.

Former State Department Official, interviewed by author, requesting anonymity, 9 December 2000, Carlisle, PA.

Gardener, Dan. "How 'victory' in the Drug War has left Colombia in ruins: the U.S. boasted that defeating Colombia's cartels would end the illegal drug trade. Instead, things got worse." <u>The Ottawa Citizen</u>, 6 September 2000. p. A1.

Golden, Tim, "Colombia and Copters and Clash Over Choice." <u>New York Times</u>, 6 March 2000, sec A. p. 6.

Gutierrez, Pedro Ruz and E. A. Torriero, "U.S. Aid Bill For Colombia Creates Jitters." <u>The Sun-Sentinel (Fort Lauderdale)</u>, 2 July 2000, p. 1A.

_____, "Outsourcing the Drug War." <u>The Orlando Sentinel</u>, 19 September 2000. p. 1.

Kotler, Jared, "Military Suffers Heavy Losses in Colombia Fighting." The Associated Press, 20 September 2000. Available from <<u>http://ap.com/ ap/breaking/mga3cxfqkec.html</u>. Internet. Assessed 22 October 2000.

Kurian, George T, Datapedia<u> of the Untied States 1790-2000</u>. (Lanham, MD: Bernan Press, 1994), p 155.

Leshner, Alan. "Addiction is a Brain Disease, and It Matters." Science 278 (3 October 1997): 45-47.

McHugh, Jane, "FIRED." The Army Times, 20 November 2000, p. 8.

Nestler, Eric J. and George K. Agha_anian. "Molecular and Cellular Basis of Addiction." Science 278 (3 October 1997): 58-63.

Nyhan, David, "Colombian drug war: it's Vietnam all over again." The Gazette (Montreal), 13 July 2000, Editorial/Op-ed, p. b-3.

Reza, H.G., "Drug Runners Arrested at Border Often Go Free; Smuggling: Crackdown Leads to More Seizures, but Jail Overcrowding and Clashing Priorities Force Suspects' Release." The Los Angeles Times, 12 May1996, p 1.

Robberson, Tod. "Clinton launches Colombia aid plan: 'This is not Vietnam,' president says." The Dallas Morning News, 31 August 2000, p. 1A.

Schmitt, Eric, "$1.3 Billion Voted To Fight Drug War Among Colombians." The New York Times, 30 June 2000, sec. A, p.1.

Seper, Jerry, "Big Guns Are Back In Aerial Drug War." Washington Times, 21 September 2000, p.8.

Shine, Barbara, "Some Cocaine Abusers Fare Better With Cognitive-Behavioral Therapy, Others With 12-Step Program," NIDA Notes 15-1 (No date). Available from <http://www.drugabuse.gov/ Nida_notes/nnvol15n1/cocaine.html>. Internet. Accessed 27 October 2000.

Stocker, Steven, "Men and Women in Drug Abuse Treatment Relapse at Different Rates and for Different Reasons." NIDA Notes 13-4 (No date). Available from <http://www.drugabuse.gov /Nida_notes/nnvol13n/relapse.html>. Internet. Accessed 27 October 2000.

"Underwater Operations." Associated Press, 7 September 2000. Available from<
    http://www.abcnews.go.com/sections/world/dailynews/colombia000907.html >.
    Internet. Accessed 1 October 2000.

U.S. Drug Enforcement Administration Intelligence Division, Strategic Intelligence. Coca
    Cultivation and Cocaine Processing: An Overview, September 1993. Available
    from <http://www.druglibrary.org/schaffer govpubs/cocccp.htm>. Internet.
    Accessed 11 February 2001.

U.S. National Institute on Drug Abuse, INFOFAX High School and Youth Trends 13565.
    Available from <http://www.drugabuse.gov/infofax/nationaltrends.html>. Internet.
    Accessed 27 October 2000.

U.S. National Institute on Drug Abuse, INFOFAX National Trends 13567. Available from
    <http://www.drugabuse.gov/infofax/nationaltrends.html>. Internet. Accessed 27
    October 2000.

U.S. National Institute on Drug Abuse, INFOFAX Treatment Trends 13569. Available
    from <http://www.drugabuse.gov/infofax/nationaltrends.html>. Internet.
    Accessed 27 October 2000.

U.S. Office of National Drug Control Policy, Annual Report of the National Drug Control
    Strategy: An Overview." Available from <http://www.white
    housedurgpolicy.gov/ndcs00/chap1.html>. Internet. Accessed 22 January 2001.

U.S. Office of National Drug Control Policy, Strategic Goals and Objectives of the 2000
    National Drug Control Strategy." Available from <http://www.white
    housedurgpolicy.gov/ndcs00/chap1.html>. Internet. Accessed 22 January 2001.

Wickelgren, Ingrid, "Getting the Brain's Attention." Science 278 (3 October 1997): 35.

Zickler, Patrick, "Combining Drug Counseling Methods Proves Effective in Treating Cocaine Addiction." <u>NIDA Notes</u> 14-5 (No date). Available from <<u>http://www.drugabuse.gov /Nida_notes/nnvol14n5/combining.html</u>>. Internet. Accessed 27 October 2000.

_____, "High-Dose Methadone Improves Treatment Outcomes." <u>NIDA Notes</u> 14-5 (No date). Available from <<u>http://www.drugabuse.gov/Nida_notes /nnvol14n5/highdose.html</u>>. Internet. Accessed 27 October 2000.

_____, "Coping Skills Help Patients Recognize and Resist The Urge to Use Cocaine." <u>NIDA Notes</u> 13-6 (No date). Available from<<u>http://www.drugabuse.gov/Nida_notes/nnvol13n6 /coping.html</u>>. Internet. Accessed 27 October 2000.